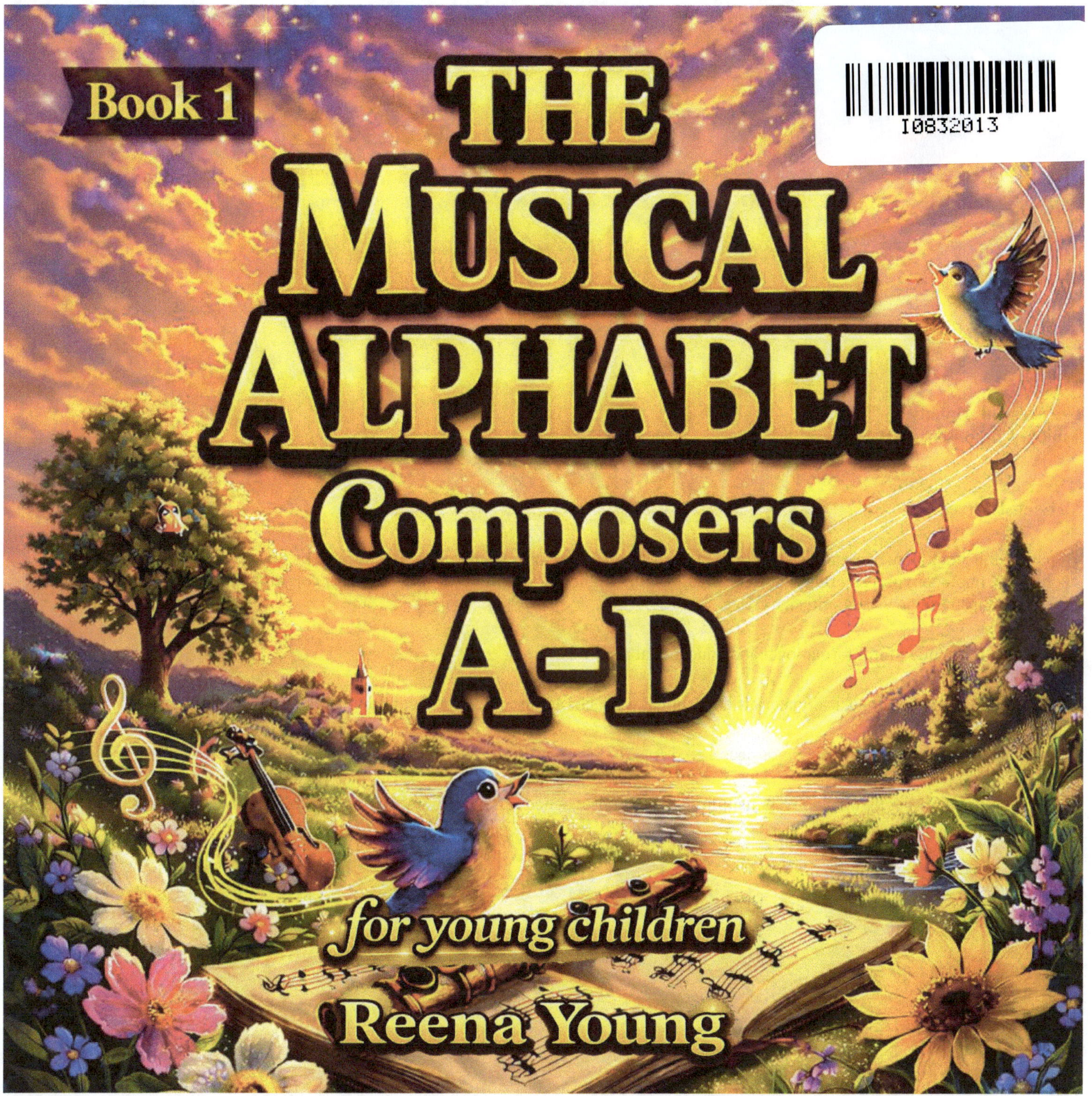
Book 1
THE MUSICAL ALPHABET
Composers
A-D
for young children
Reena Young

The Musical Alphabet
Book 1: Composers A–D

This edition is intended for informational and educational purposes.

All illustrations, texts, and musical materials are original works or are used with proper authorization.

Any resemblance to real people, living or deceased, is purely historical and educational in nature.

The author and publisher assume no responsibility for any consequences arising from the use of the information contained in this book.

Publisher: IVY Music Publishing
Author: Reena Young
United States of America

ISBN: 978-1-972314-00-5

This series of books,

The Musical Alphabet,

is dedicated to my dear students.

Thank you for everything you have taught me!

With love,

Reena Young

Welcome to the wonderful world of music!

In this book, you will meet twelve great composers whose names begin with the letters **A** to **D**.

Their music comes from many countries and many centuries, yet it still inspires people all over the world.

Scan the QR codes, listen to the music, and discover how composers turn sounds into stories.

Happy reading and listening!

Contents:

D

About the book:

It has long been known that classical music has a beneficial influence on a child's development. Yet behind these words lies not dry science, but a true and living miracle.

Music is alive.

It exists not only in the past, in textbooks, or in concert halls. It sounds around us every day — in films and cartoons, in theaters and games, at home by the piano, in headphones, and sometimes even in silence.

Classical music is not merely a beautiful sound. It is a living language of feelings, images, and moods that gently touches the human soul.

When a child listens to good music, tiny lights seem to turn on inside the brain. New connections are formed. Memory and attention grow. Imagination and speech develop. The ability to feel, to empathize, and to understand the world becomes deeper and richer.

The earlier music appears in a child's life, the deeper its roots grow. In early childhood, the foundations of future abilities are laid — intellectual, emotional, and creative.

That is why this series of books was created in a special way.

From the very beginning, it was conceived as a living musical ecosystem for children — an entire world where classical music becomes close, understandable, and beloved from the very first steps.

In these books, there is no dry listing of dates and complicated terms. Instead, the book invites the child into a space where composers become friends, musical works turn into stories, and listening becomes an exciting journey filled with discovery and joy.

Gradually, a natural interest in the world of beautiful, meaningful sounds emerges. This interest can support an active and curious mind throughout life, helping to preserve clarity of thought, inner culture, and a sense of wonder.

A special role in this process is played by the formation of taste. By hearing good music from early childhood, a child learns to distinguish the genuine from the superficial, to feel the expressiveness of melody, the warmth of harmony, and the power of rhythm.

Such taste becomes a quiet and reliable compass for a lifetime.

This Musical Alphabet was born from a simple but important idea: good music has no age. That is why different eras and styles live side by side in these books. Here you will meet great composers of the past as well as composers closer to our own time. All good music stands here as equal, because music speaks to people in the universal language of feelings.

From the very beginning, the author wished to avoid the impression that classical music is something distant, complicated, or meant only for a few specialists. Music can be beautiful, exciting, playful, mysterious, or solemn — and all of this is music.

Each book in this series may be opened at any page. You may begin with a composer whose name starts with the same letter as your child's name. You may start with music already familiar from a cartoon or a film. Or you may simply follow curiosity.

The books intentionally provide only a small amount of information about each composer. At this stage, it is enough to know the composer's name, recognize their music, and see their portraits. This is often enough for the first spark of interest to appear.

If a child later wishes to learn more, a vast world of knowledge is always open in libraries and on the Internet.

Some of the musical works presented in the book consist of several movements. For a first acquaintance, it is enough to listen to the first movement. The rest may be discovered later, if desired.

The books include links and QR codes leading to musical videos on YouTube. The author tried to select versions without advertisements, but unfortunately, this is not always possible. Therefore, it is recommended that adults help the child skip advertisements and remain nearby during listening.

These books do not aim to teach everything at once. Its purpose is much simpler and more important — **to begin a friendship with music**.

If, after this Alphabet, your child wishes to listen, to play, to ask questions, and to discover more, then the books have fulfilled their most important purpose.

May this book become the first doorway into a great musical world — a world where every sound may turn into a small miracle.

With love for music and children,

Reena Young

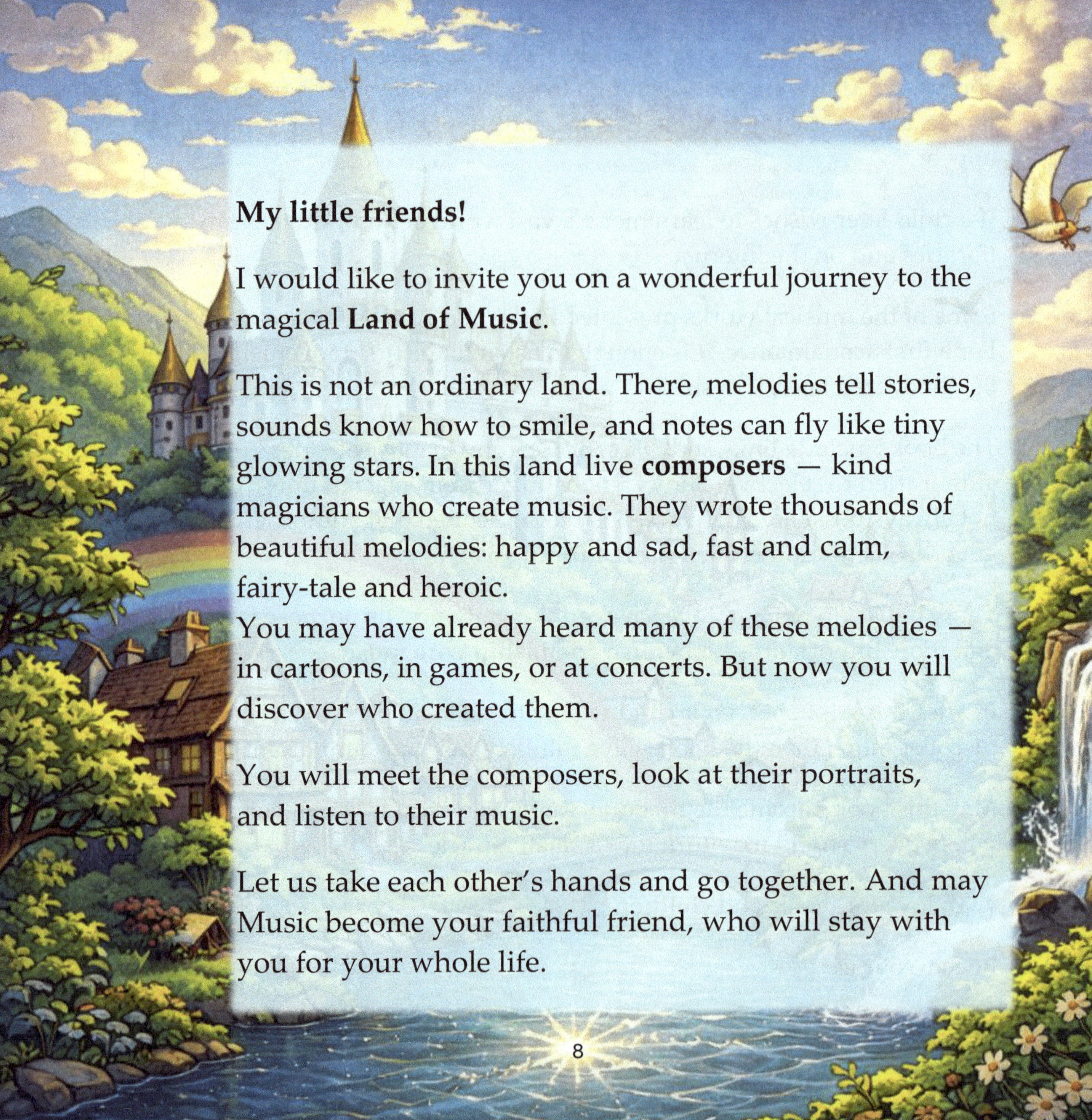

My little friends!

I would like to invite you on a wonderful journey to the magical **Land of Music**.

This is not an ordinary land. There, melodies tell stories, sounds know how to smile, and notes can fly like tiny glowing stars. In this land live **composers** — kind magicians who create music. They wrote thousands of beautiful melodies: happy and sad, fast and calm, fairy-tale and heroic.
You may have already heard many of these melodies — in cartoons, in games, or at concerts. But now you will discover who created them.

You will meet the composers, look at their portraits, and listen to their music.

Let us take each other's hands and go together. And may Music become your faithful friend, who will stay with you for your whole life.

Albéniz

1860 - 1909

Isaac Albéniz was born in sunny **Spain**.
From an early age, he loved music and learned to play the piano.

He also traveled a lot and listened to how life sounds all around him: songs, dances, the ringing of **guitars**, and the lively noise of streets and festivals.

Albéniz became famous for writing **piano** music that features hot Spanish dance **rhythms**. His music is cheerful and lively, as if inviting you on a journey to Spain.

Listen to the piece **"Asturias"** from the **"Spanish Suite."**

On the piano, it sounds like a dance. Asturias is the name of a place in Spain. It is performed by **Anastasia Huppmann** from **Austria**.

https://www.youtube.com/watch?v=8aKtGrjFVhl&list=RD8aKtGrjFVhl&start_radio=1

Albinoni

1671 - 1751

Tomaso Albinoni lived in **Italy**, in the beautiful city on the water — **Venice**. He loved music very much and wrote it so that it would be singing and melodic, like a song.

He played the **violin** and the **harpsichord**, an old instrument similar to the piano. Albinoni's music flows smoothly, like a boat gliding across the water. In Venice, boats are called gondolas, and you can still see them there today.

Listen to the beautiful "**Adagio.**"
The word "adagio" comes from Italian and means "slow and calm" music. It is performed by the **Copernicus Chamber Orchestra** from **Poland.**

https://www.youtube.com/watch?v=_eLU5W1vc8Y&list=RD_eLU5W1vc8Y&start_radio=1

Anderson

1908 - 1975

Leroy Anderson was an **American** composer and **conductor**. He loved writing cheerful, playful music that tells funny stories without using words.

Many of his pieces sound like little musical cartoons. Leroy Anderson showed that classical music can be fun, surprising, and full of imagination.

One of his most famous works is **"The Typewriter,"** a song where the sounds of a real typewriter become part of the music.

It is performed by the **Brandenburg Symphoniker** from **Germany.**

https://www.youtube.com/watch?v=nW8dGwa2zRw

Bach

1685 - 1750

Johann Sebastian Bach lived in **Germany** more than 300 years ago. He loved music very much and could play many instruments: the **organ**, the **harpsichord**, the **violin**, and even the **flute**. Most often, Bach played the organ in church.

Bach wrote a lot of church music, but he also composed cheerful pieces for celebrations and concerts.

Bach's music is loved and performed all over the world even 300 years later.

When Bach grew older, he began to lose his sight after a difficult eye operation.

But even then, he did not stop composing music — he heard it with his heart.

Listen to his famous ***"Toccata and Fugue in D minor"*** for organ. It is very solemn and a little mysterious music. It sounds like music of outer space.

https://www.youtube.com/watch?v=FHNLdHe8uxY
A **"Toccata"** is fast, brilliant music in which the composer seems to show how cleverly and beautifully fingers can run across the keys. A **"Fugue"** is a musical game of voices. It is performed by **Xavier Varnus** from **Canada**.

Beethoven

1770 - 1827

Ludwig van Beethoven was born in **Germany**, just like Bach.
From childhood, Beethoven practiced the piano a great deal.
He could sit at the instrument for a long time, playing again and again.

Beethoven became a very skilled pianist and often performed in concerts. He also wrote music for many instruments and for large orchestras.

When Beethoven became an adult, he began to lose his hearing. But he continued to compose music and did not give up.

Listen to one of Beethoven's **symphonies**. In it, you will hear a famous rhythm: **"ta-ta-ta-TAM."** Beethoven said that this is how "fate knocks at the door." The music sounds bold and powerful, as if saying, "Do not be afraid. You can do it!"

It is performed by a symphony orchestra from **Germany**.

https://www.youtube.com/watch?v=7eOaliHB58U

Brahms

1833 - 1897

Johannes Brahms was a **German** composer and pianist who loved creating beautiful, warm, and thoughtful music. When he was still a boy, he practiced the piano for many hours a day and even played in cafés to help support his family.

Brahms wrote songs, piano pieces, symphonies, and also cheerful dances inspired by folk music.

Over time, Brahms became famous for music full of feeling. His music often sounds warm, noble, and very heartfelt — like a kind story told through sounds. And sometimes Brahms's music is very cheerful and dance-like.

Listen to two of Brahms's **Hungarian Dances**. This music is very famous, and you may have already heard it. It is performed by the **Youth Symphony Orchestra from Poland**.

https://www.youtube.com/watch?v=O192eo9zbT4

Chopin

1810 - 1849

Frédéric Chopin was born in **Żelazowa Wola**, near **Warsaw**, in **Poland**. From an early age, he showed extraordinary musical talent and began composing. He studied in Warsaw and quickly became known as a brilliant pianist.

As a young man, Chopin left Poland and settled in **Paris**, **France**, where he spent most of his life. There, he became famous both as a performer and as a composer. Unlike many composers of his time, he wrote almost exclusively for the piano.

His music is poetic, expressive, and full of deep feeling. It often reflects the spirit of his homeland — Polish dances such as **mazurkas** and **polonaises** appear in many of his works.

Listen to Chopin's **Mazurka** performed by a student of **Dr. Hall** from **BachScholar**.
https://www.youtube.com/watch?v=DRiY7CRdilU

Clara Schumann

1819 - 1896

Clara Schumann was born in **Leipzig, Germany**.

From a very early age, she showed extraordinary musical talent. Her father was a piano teacher and carefully guided her musical education.

Clara practiced many hours every day and soon became one of the most remarkable young pianists in Europe.

Clara was not only a pianist but also a composer.

She wrote piano pieces, songs, chamber music, and a piano **concerto**.

Although in her time women composers were often not taken seriously, Clara proved that talent and dedication have no limits.

Listen to Clara Schumann's **Three Romances for Violin and Piano,** performed by the **Esbjerg Ensemble**.

https://www.youtube.com/watch?v=yJFcJOFwtE4

Debussy

1862 - 1918

Claude Debussy was born and grew up in **France**.

He studied music in Paris and, from an early age, dreamed of creating beautiful sounds.

Claude Debussy was friends with painters and deeply loved visual art.

He wrote his music the way an artist paints a picture — as if he were painting sounds with colors.

Debussy's music is like the sea, drifting clouds, moonlit evenings, and quiet dreams. He created a new musical style in which mood and the beauty of sound are most important. **"Clair de Lune"** ("Moonlight") is one of Debussy's most famous piano pieces. It is performed here by **Steve Anderson** from the **USA**.

https://www.youtube.com/watch?v=YNGLDB9Y7Lo&list=RDYNGLDB9Y7Lo&start_radio=1

Delibes

1836 - 1891

Léo Delibes was a **French** composer who became especially famous for his music for ballet and opera.

From childhood, he loved to sing, play the piano, and compose beautiful melodies.

Léo Delibes knew how to create bright, fairy-tale music that is easy to imagine dancing, toys, and magical characters.

Delibes composed three ballets and several operas.

Watch the **Variation** from the ballet ***Coppélia*.** It is written in a waltz rhythm.

In ballet, the word **"variation"** means a short solo dance.

Coppélia is the name of the ballet's heroine — a beautiful and mysterious doll-like girl.

The Royal Opera House, Covent Garden; danced by **Natalia Osipova**.

https://www.youtube.com/watch?v=-c1htjAp5nY

Dukas

1865 - 1935

Paul Dukas was a **French** composer who loved fairy tales, fantasy, and magical stories. From childhood, he studied music, played the piano, and composed many pieces.

Paul Dukas's most famous work is the **symphonic poem *The Sorcerer's Apprentice.***

It tells the story of a boy, a magician's apprentice, who tries to use magic without permission and ends up causing a real flood! The music sounds mysterious at times, funny at others, and sometimes very energetic — like a fairy tale come to life.

Listen to **the Gewandhaus Orchestra perform** Paul Dukas' **"The Sorcerer's Apprentice".**

https://www.youtube.com/watch?v=O_bdguZEl8Q

Dvořák

1841 - 1904

Antonín Dvořák was a **Czech** composer. He was born in a small village in Bohemia.

As a child, he loved music and learned to play the violin. He loved listening to folk songs and dances from his homeland and later incorporated them into his music.

Dvořák traveled to the United States, where he was inspired by American music. He wrote his famous **Symphony "From the New World,"** where he created melodies that feel like American folk songs.

Listen to: Antonín Dvořák — **Slavonic Dance No. 2** performed by the **Gewandhausorchester** from **Germany**.

At the beginning, you hear a slow, singing melody that feels like a gentle Slavic folk song, full of warmth and quiet emotion. Then the music becomes lighter and more dance-like, as if people begin to move and celebrate together.

https://www.youtube.com/watch?v=Zf-Z9YLz3MQ&list=RDZf-Z9YLz3MQ&start_radio=1

Can you find them? (Answers on the last page)

1. a church
2. a piano
3. a violinist
4. a gondola
5. a letter D
6. a castle
7. the mountains
8. a ballerina
9. a conductor
10. a trumpet
11. a letter A
12. a harpsichord
13. a typewriter
14. a church organ
15. a river
16. a magician
17. a letter B
18. a guitar
19. a mechanical doll
20. a violin
21. an American flag
22. a ballet stage
23. a letter C
24. a village
25. a carriage
26. a cathedral

Musical Questions (Answers on the last page)

1. Which composer wrote music for piano?

2. Which composer lived in Venice?

3. Which composer almost lost his hearing?

4. Which composer wrote music for ballet?

5. How many composers were born in Germany?

6. Which composer wrote piano music inspired by Spanish dances?

7. Which composers lived in France?

Appendix 1.

Additional works to enjoy on YouTube.

1. The best of **Albéniz**

Best of Isaac Albéniz - Classical Guitar Compilation

2. The best of **Albinoni**

https://youtu.be/2DL5YpEobO0?si=z6_Ekreyy-zsJ4s4

3. The best of **Leroy Anderson**

PAPEL DE LIJA (SANDPAPER). Leroy Anderson. - YouTube

4. The best of **Bach**

https://youtu.be/6JQm5aSjX6g?si=Hpz_ad7StUov28Le

5. The best of **Beethoven**

50 Best of Beethoven

6. The best of **Brahms**

The Best of Brahms - YouTube

6a. **Brahms'** ***"Lullaby"***

https://youtu.be/T6nb35I9w-8?si=gt5o6On555vvG776

7. The best of **Chopin**

Best of Chopin - 5 Most Popular Pieces - YouTube

8. The best of **Clara Schumann**

Clara Schumann: Piano Concerto in A minor, Op.7 - Alice Burla & SJSO - YouTube

9. The best of **Debussy**

https://youtu.be/UETuJ2LXJWQ?si=E2sSC8p1AzAsCPxG

10. The best of **Delibes**

https://youtu.be/zbeFZ7sSQqc?si=smCPXxKa2Ahnf-wB

11.The best of **Dukas**

https://www.youtube.com/watch?v=51lPkJWWtMM&list=RD51lPkJWWtMM&start_radio=1

There is also the famous Disney animated film *The Sorcerer's Apprentice,* which helps children truly hear and feel this music.

12.The best of **Dvořák**

https://www.youtube.com/results?search_query=the+best+of+dvorak

Appendix 2.

More Music to Explore

If you enjoyed discovering these composers, here are more beautiful pieces you can listen to. Try to find them on YouTube and choose the performance you like most.

Isaac Albéniz

• *Asturias (Leyenda)*
— strong, guitar-like sound, full of Spanish energy

• *Granada*
— gentle and warm, like an evening in Spain

• *Sevilla*
— lively and rhythmic, almost like a dance

Tomaso Albinoni

• *Adagio in G minor*
— slow, emotional, very expressive

• *Oboe Concerto in D minor (2nd movement)*
— calm and flowing, with a beautiful oboe melody

• *Oboe Concerto in F major (1st movement)*
— light, elegant, and cheerful

Leroy Anderson

• *Sleigh Ride*
— bright winter music, like a joyful snowy day

• *The Syncopated Clock*
— ticking rhythms that feel like a funny clock

Johann Sebastian Bach

• *Minuet in G Major*
— simple, clear, and elegant

• *Air on the G String*
— calm and flowing, very peaceful

• *Brandenburg Concerto No. 3 (1st movement)*
— lively and energetic, like music in motion

• *Prelude in C Major (The Well-Tempered Clavier)*
— gentle and steady, like quiet thinking

Ludwig van Beethoven

• *Für Elise*
— light and familiar, with a gentle mood

• *Symphony No. 6 "Pastoral" (1st movement)*
— peaceful and bright, inspired by nature

• *Moonlight Sonata (1st movement)*
— soft, slow, and deeply expressive

Johannes Brahms

• *Intermezzo in A Major, Op. 118 No. 2*
— warm, reflective, like a quiet conversation

• *Symphony No. 3 (3rd movement)*
— gentle, flowing, with a soft, nostalgic mood

• *Clarinet Quintet (2nd movement)*
— calm and expressive, with a rich, mellow sound

Frédéric Chopin

• *Nocturne in E-flat Major, Op. 9 No. 2*
— calm and singing, like a quiet night

• *Prelude in E Minor, Op. 28 No. 4*
— slow and thoughtful, with a gentle sadness

• *Waltz in A Minor (B. 150)*
— simple and expressive, like a personal story

Clara Schumann

• *Nocturne in F Major, Op. 6 No. 2*
— soft and flowing, with a peaceful mood

• *Piano Trio in G Minor, Op. 17 (2nd movement)*
— gentle and expressive, like a quiet conversation

Claude Debussy

• *Arabesque No. 1*
— light and flowing, like a gentle breeze

• *The Little Shepherd (Children's Corner)*
— simple and calm, like a quiet moment

• *La fille aux cheveux de lin (The Girl with the Flaxen Hair)*
— soft and warm, with a singing melody

Léo Delibes

• *Lakmé – Bell Song*
— bright and sparkling, with a very high voice

• *Coppélia – Mazurka*
— lively and rhythmic, like a character dance

Paul Dukas

• *La Péri – Fanfare*
— bold and brilliant, like a musical signal

Antonín Dvořák

• *Symphony No. 9 "From the New World" (1st movement)*
— strong and full of energy

• *Serenade for Strings (1st movement)*
— warm and flowing, very friendly in sound

• *Songs My Mother Taught Me*
— gentle and expressive, like a folk song

Our journey through the Land of Music continues.
In the next book, new composers and new musical stories are waiting for you.

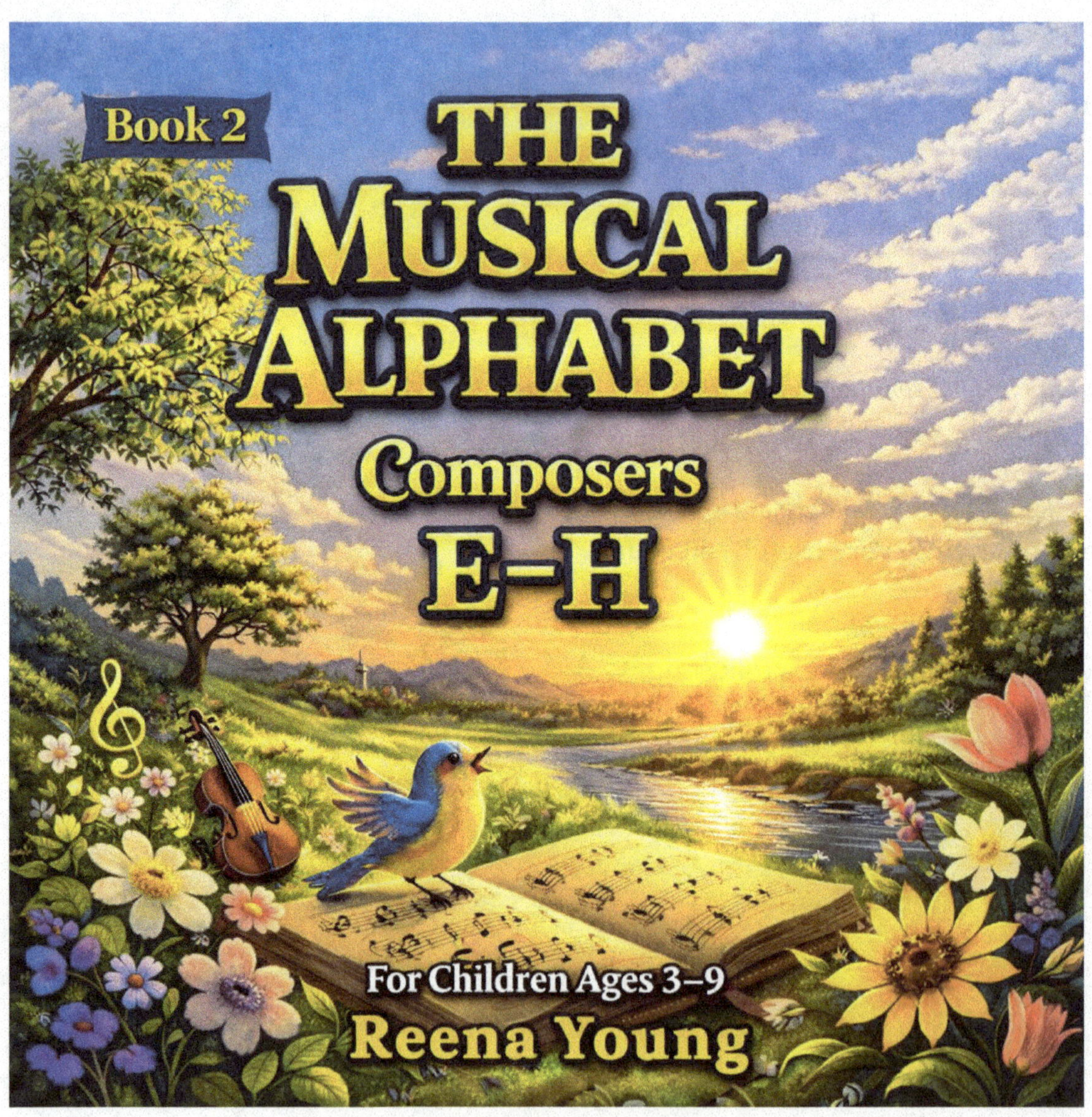

COLLECT THE MUSICAL ALPHABET SERIES

Each book opens a new door into the world of music.

BOOK 1 **Composers A – D:**

Albéniz
Albinoni
Anderson
Bach
Beethoven
Brahms
Chopin
Clara Schumann
Debussy
Delibes
Dukas
Dvořák

BOOK 2 **Composers E – H:**

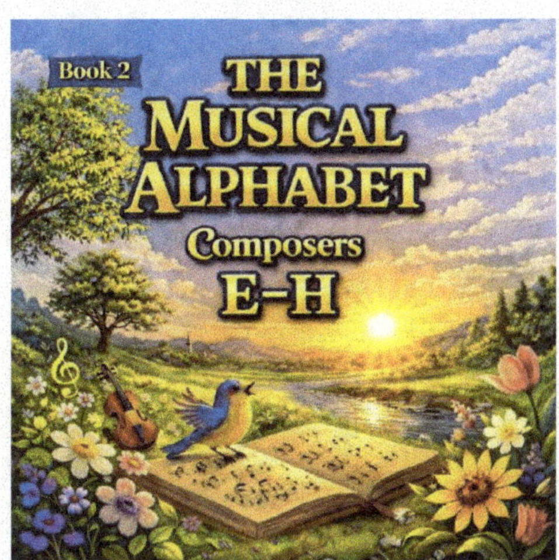

Elgar
Enescu
Erik Satie
De Falla
Fauré
Franck
Gershwin
Gluck

Granados

Grieg

Handel

Horner

- -

BOOK 3 Composers I – L: Ibert

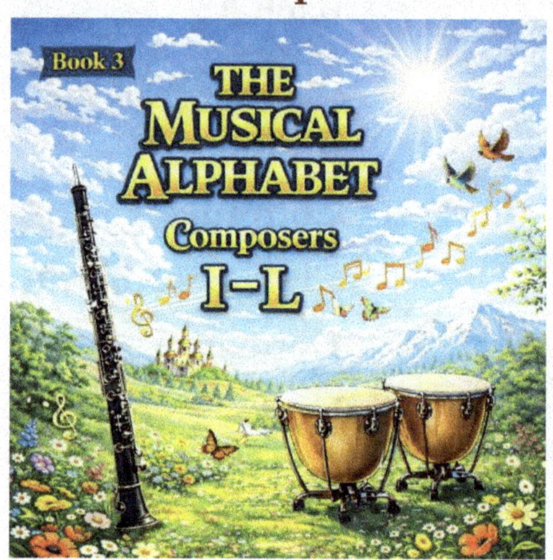

Irving Berlin

Ives

Jean Sibelius

Joseph Haydn

Jules Massenet

Kálmán

Kabalevsky

Khachaturian

Kreisler

Lehár

Liszt

- -

BOOK 4 Composers M – P:

Mancini

Mendelssohn

Milhaud

Morricone

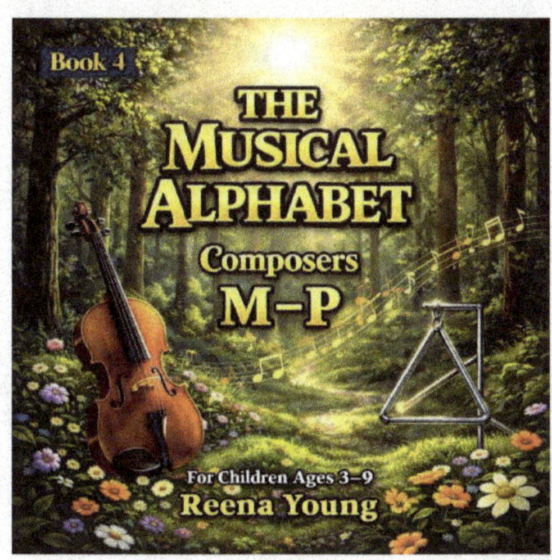

Mozart
Nino Rota
Offenbach
Ogiński
Pachelbel
Paganini
Prokofiev
Puccini

BOOK 5 Composers Q – S:

Coming in 2026

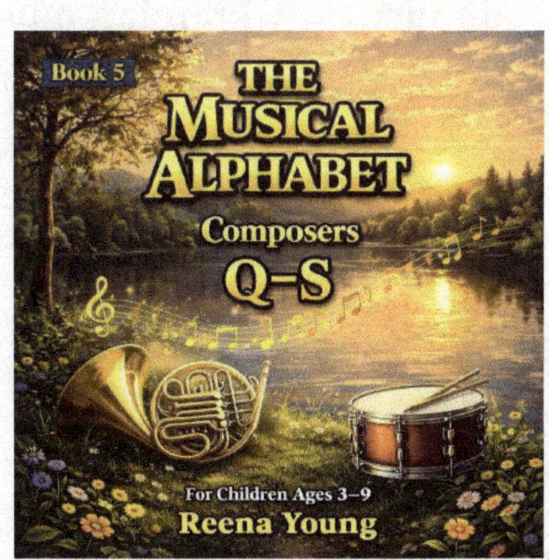

Quilter
Rachmaninoff
Ravel
Rimsky-Korsakov
Rossini
Saint-Saëns
Schumann
Shore
Shostakovich
Sousa
Strauss
Stravinsky

BOOK 6 Composers T – W:

Coming in 2026

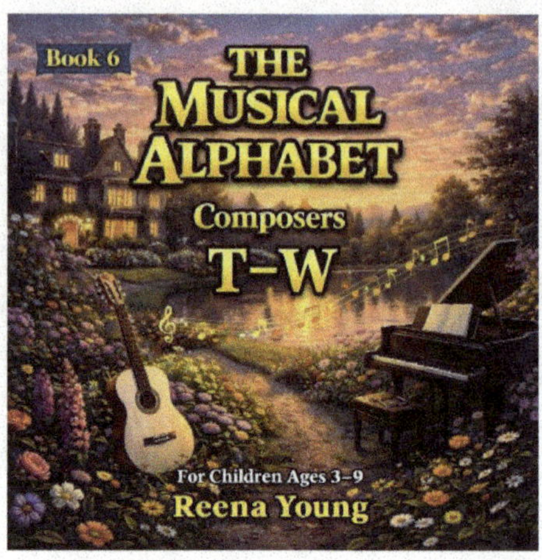

- Tartini
- Tchaikovsky
- Telemann
- Torelli
- Vanhal
- Verdi
- Villa-Lobos
- Vivaldi
- Wagner
- Webber
- Wieniawski
- Williams

Bonus: Ukrainian music

BOOK 7 Composers X – Z:

Coming in 2026

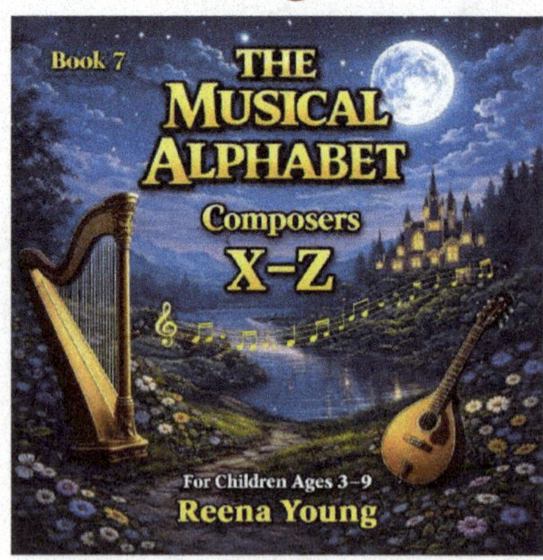

- Xaver Scharwenka
- Xian Xinghai
- Yanni
- Yamada
- Yoko Kanno
- Ysaÿe
- Zdeněk Fibich
- Zélenka
- Zieleński
- Zelter

Zimbalist

Zimmer

BOOK 8 **Musical Instruments**

BOOK 9 **Genres and Forms of Music**

BOOK 10 **The Great Performers**

BOOK 11 **Music for the Screen**

BOOK 12 **The Ages of Music**

Appendix 3.
Glossary

Adagio
A musical term meaning *slow and calm*. Music played adagio feels peaceful and expressive.

Ballerina
A female ballet dancer. She performs graceful dances on stage, often wearing special pointe shoes.

Ballet
A type of theater performance where a story is told through dance and music.

Ballet variation
A short solo dance in a ballet that shows the dancer's skill and character.

Chamber orchestra
A small orchestra with fewer musicians than a symphony orchestra. It usually performs in smaller halls.

Composer
A person who writes music.

Concerto
A musical piece in which a solo instrument plays alongside an orchestra.

Conductor
The person who leads the orchestra and helps all the musicians play together.

Conservatory
A special school where students study music, singing, and musical instruments.

Ensemble
A small group of musicians playing music together.

Flute
A wind instrument that makes sound when the player blows across a small opening.

Fugue
A musical composition where the same theme is repeated and developed by different voices or instruments.

Guitar
A string instrument that is usually played by plucking or strumming the strings.

Harpsichord
An early keyboard instrument from the Baroque period. Its strings are plucked rather than struck, as on a piano.

Mazurka
A lively Polish dance in triple rhythm.

Opera
A theatrical performance in which the story is sung rather than spoken.

Operetta
A lighter and shorter type of opera, often with funny or romantic stories.

Organ
A large keyboard instrument usually found in churches. It produces sound using air and pipes.

Oratorio
A large musical work for orchestra, choir, and solo singers, usually based on a religious story.

Piano
A keyboard instrument where strings are struck by small hammers when the keys are pressed.

Polonaise
A stately Polish dance in triple time.

Prelude
A short musical piece that introduces a larger work or sets a mood.

Prodigy
A child with extraordinary talent, especially in music.

Rhythm
The pattern of beats in music — the way sounds are organized in time.

Romance
A lyrical and expressive musical piece, often gentle and emotional.

Sonata
A musical composition, usually written for one instrument or a small group of instruments.

Suite
A collection of short musical pieces played one after another.

Symphonic orchestra
A very large orchestra with strings, woodwinds, brass, and percussion instruments.

Symphonic poem
An orchestral piece that tells a story or describes an idea, a poem, or a scene.

Symphony
A large musical work for orchestra, usually made of several movements.

Toccata

A fast and brilliant musical piece that shows the performer's skill.

Variation (music)

A musical form where a theme is repeated several times, but each time it is changed in a new way.

Violin

A small string instrument played with a bow.

The last question: Which composer(s) did you like the most?

Did your child enjoy this musical journey?

I would truly love to hear your thoughts. Your review helps other children and parents discover this book and begin their journey into the world of music.

For your convenience, simply scan the QR code below to go directly to the review page on Amazon or use the link.

Thank you for being part of this story.

With love,
Reena Young

https://www.amazon.com/dp/1972314009

Can you find them?

1. Pages 15, 23,25, 27, 32, 39, 47, 55, 57
2. 9, 12, 28, 36, 40, 41
3. 20, 29, 57
4. 15, 17
5. 42, 46, 50, 54
6. 9, 11, 39, 52
7. 11, 13, 32, 56
8. 48, 49
9. 18, 20, 29
10. 9, 20
11. 10, 14, 18
12. 16
13. 21
14. 24,
15. 32, 35, 39, 43, 47, 51, 55, 56
16. 52
17. 22, 26, 30
18. 9, 13
19. 49
20. 16, 20, 29, 37, 41, 46, 54, 57
21. 18, 19
22. 48, 49
23. 32, 38
24. 32, 35, 55
25. 31, 47,
26. 15, 23, 25, 27, 47,

Musical questions:

1. Chopin
2. Albinoni
3. Beethoven
4. Delibes
5. Four: Bach, Beethoven, Brahms, and Clara Schumann
6. Albéniz
7. Chopin, Debussy, Delibes, Dukas

The other books by Reena Young

Skillful Little Fingers is a preparatory piano method designed to help young students feel confident and at ease at the keyboard from the very beginning.

Through carefully structured exercises, children become familiar with both white and black keys early on, reducing fear and building natural coordination. Special attention is given to black-key groups, Chopin's Position, B major, and chromatic preparation, so that when music theory appears later, the hands already feel at home.

The book is intentionally flexible. It is not intended to replace any method chosen by the teacher, but rather to complement and enrich existing piano instruction. Exercises can be integrated freely into lessons, adapted to individual students, and used alongside any curriculum.

Designed for young hands and developing minds, **Skillful Little Fingers** supports a calm, confident, and joyful start at the piano.

Skillful Little Fingers – Book II continues the journey toward confident, natural piano technique.

This book builds on the foundation established in Book I and gently expands the student's experience across the keyboard. Scales, patterns, and coordinated movements are introduced in a clear and practical way, without rushing into abstract theory.

One important goal of this book is to help the hands feel comfortable on both white and black keys. Through consistent finger patterns and carefully designed exercises, the keyboard becomes familiar rather than intimidating.

The material in this book is not meant to replace any existing piano method. Instead, it is designed to complement the teacher's chosen approach and support technical development alongside repertoire.

Skillful Little Fingers focuses on what matters most at this stage:

relaxed hands, balanced movement, and growing confidence at the keyboard.

www.ingramcontent.com/pod-product-compliance
Lightning Source LLC
LaVergne TN
LVHW081420110826
845149LV00010B/1808

* 9 7 8 1 9 7 2 3 1 4 0 0 5 *